Buying Real Estate in Massachusetts

A legal guide to having the best closing

By David R. Rocheford, Jr., Esq.

ISBN: 978-1533091185

REALTOR® is a federally registered collective membership mark which identifies a real estate professional who is a Member of the NATIONAL ASSOCIATION OF REALTORS® and subscribes to its strict Code of Ethics.

DISCLAIMER
This publication is intended to be informational only. No legal advice is being given, and no attorney-client relationship is intended to be created by reading this material. If you are facing legal issues, whether criminal or civil, seek professional legal counsel to get your questions answered.

Additional copies are available at special quantity discounts for bulk purchases for sales promotions, premiums, fundraising, and educational use.

For more information, please contact:
David Rocheford
156 Hamilton Street
Leominster, MA 01453. or call (978) 728-5104
Contact the author directly at David Rocheford at
davidr@thebestclosings.com

Contents

My first piece of advice?

First off, it is important to know that you don't have to try to reinvent the wheel on your real estate transaction. Buying and selling real estate has been happening for ages. Even though every piece of real estate is unique and every transaction is different, most aspects of the process are anticipated and predictable. With the right type of counsel, the home buying experience can be very simple and pleasant.

Next, I would say not to rely strictly on advice from people who aren't in the business and especially not on the general guidance from the Internet. If you depend on unreliable sources, you are likely to receive poor and erroneous advice. It is vital that you work with experienced, active, and local real estate professionals.

The best way to find YOUR real estate team

A good place to start is to ask friends, family members, or co-workers who may have recently purchased a home. Ask them to share their experiences. They will either tell you that their team did a fantastic job, or they will immediately begin to tell you what went wrong. Naturally, you want to work with a team you know, like, and trust; it's the key to any relationship.

When you are looking for a real estate attorney, look for one that focuses strictly on real estate matters. There are many,

many attorneys practicing in all of aspects of law. Unfortunately, I frequently see situations where a simple transaction becomes a mess as a result of choosing the wrong attorney. I recall a recent transaction where the buyer had an attorney who was making mistake after mistake throughout the transaction. I didn't understand why at first, but shortly after, when I explored the firm's website, I saw that real estate was #8 on the list of various legal matters the firm handles. Number one was bankruptcy, and then there were wills, trusts, probates, and so on and so on. The website showed this little sentence that stated, "We do real estate," which is fine, but more often than not, firms that take on matters outside of their areas of expertise tend to underserve their clients. You are not going to make an appointment with me to help you with a divorce, and if you did, I would tell you that I don't do Family Law. If you get a DUI, don't come to me because I can't help you. It's just not what I do.

The thing I CAN help you with is real estate, and if you go to my website, you will see that it is what we do. It's ALL we do. If you needed brain surgery, you would never go to an orthopedic surgeon who works on knees. While this isn't brain surgery, and it's not necessarily life or death, for most people purchasing a home represents the largest financial commitment they are ever going to make in their lives.

The difference between a Real Estate Agent/Broker and a Realtor®

Many people are unfamiliar with the real estate industry and its various terms and jargon, so it is no surprise that many people use the term Realtor®, real estate agent, and broker interchangeably, which essentially is incorrect.

A Realtor® is the term used to refer to a real estate agent who has become a member of the National Association of Realtors®. This means the agent is bound by the association's professional standards and its code of ethics. The association attempts to standardize the real estate industry by introducing high standards for its member agents to ensure that clients don't have to worry if their agent represents their best interests or not.

A real estate agent is a professional who has undertaken all of the necessary classes and passed their licensing exam to acquire a real estate license. Each state has its own licensing body, requirements, and testing, which a person must take in order to work as a real estate agent in that particular state.

A real estate broker has ventured even further in terms of real estate education and has passed the broker license exam. A broker's license allows an agent to work independently of another broker or even hire other agents to work for them.

The distinction here is that a real estate agent has to work through a real estate broker, who would be responsible for overseeing their actions and providing guidance and resources whenever necessary. A Realtor®, on the other hand, has been able to acquire membership of a prestigious association that further attests their competency and ethical responsibilities. Whenever possible, I recommend working with a real estate agent or broker who is a Realtor®. That being said, there are many outstanding and qualified real estate agents and brokers who are not Realtors®, and they do an adequate job for their clients.

The difference between a buyer's agent and a seller's agent

I highly recommend that first-time homebuyers work with buyer's agents. You can go into an advertised open house some Sunday afternoon and talk with the agent that's there, and they can help you purchase that property. However, you must understand that the agent's fiduciary responsibility lies with the seller. Anything that seller's agent says or does is going to be for the benefit of the seller of that property. Realtor® guidelines state that "the agent owes the seller client undivided loyalty, reasonable care, disclosure, obedience to lawful instructions, confidentiality and accounting. The agent must put the seller's interests first and attempt to negotiate price and terms acceptable to their seller client." It is true that they do have a common responsibility of candor and fair dealing, and obviously, they cannot be deceitful or act in a misleading manner. However, it is critical for the buyer to remember that a listing agent always represents the seller and does not represent the buyer.

When you are a first-time homebuyer, it is always in your best interest to contract with a buyer's agent, who is going to have YOUR best interest in mind. When your agent takes you to an open house or to see a property, they are going to make sure that you, the buyer, are protected. Their fiduciary responsibility is to you as their buyer client. On countless occasions I have seen buyers completely misrepresented by not having their own agent to guide and advise them.

A listing broker, or seller's agent, will be paid directly by the seller according to the commission or listing agreement they enter into with each other. Always know in advance how your buyer's agent will be compensated. Most listing brokers will offer to pay a cooperating agent a percentage of the commission. Some brokers will not. Some buyer's agents will charge the buyer a fee directly to the buyer. Obviously, the buyer's agent deserves to be paid, but you should be able to find an agent who is willing work with you and be paid on terms that are acceptable to you. Don't wait until closing to ask your buyer's agent how they will be compensated. In any event, the agent is required to disclose to you up front who they represent and how they will be compensated.

Choosing a lender

Above anything else, I always tell clients to keep it local when they are looking for a mortgage loan officer, mortgage lender, or bank. More than 90% of the transactions where I see problems are transactions where the buyer sought financing on the Internet, through an 800 number, or through a television or radio advertisement.

Working with a local credit union, bank, or mortgage broker for financing will save you a lot of stress and anxiety. The main reason for keeping it local is accountability. When you work with a national 800 number company, you get a loan "specialist" who you know nothing about. You have no idea how long he or she has been in the business or what their qualifications are. They can probably get you through the process of getting you the loan you are looking for, but it may well be the only loan that they have originated in the county within the past 10 to 20 days or more. It may also be the last transaction they originate in the area. Their next transaction may be in Florida, or the next transaction may be in New Hampshire. There is NO accountability to your other team members. Your Realtor® must deal with the short promises that the loan "specialist" may make because the loan "specialist" is sitting at a desk somewhere in California or the mid-west or who knows where. They have no skin in the game, so to say, to deliver great customer service. When they make promises that they can't deliver, it is the real estate agent and the attorney who have the reputation in the community, and they are left to deal with the issues when the dust settles.

When you work with local providers, your Realtor® is going to make sure that they perform. Because if they don't perform, the local professionals may make certain that their volume of business is diminished by spreading the word about their poor service. Reputation is paramount in this situation. An 800 number or internet lender may not care if things don't go well because their clientele comes from everywhere. For them it is not local.

Yes, your mortgage rate is important. A low rate can mean the difference between qualifying for a property you want and one you are only satisfied with. However, I always advise clients to never shop on rate alone. Rate is important, obviously, but if you have a quarter of a point difference between a local lender and a national lender, my recommendation all day long is to always take the higher rate of the local lender, even if it is going to amount to significant cash over the lifetime of the loan—possibly thousands of dollars. On the other hand, working with an unknown could result in higher varied costs up front, not to mention the stress and anxiety of not knowing if the lender can or will actually deliver.

What other advice can you expect from your team?

Your agent and loan officer may not have all of the answers for you, but it is critical that they have the resources to get the answers you need. Your team should know the steps involved and the unique aspects of the transaction. When buyers have questions like "How do I submit an offer to a corporate owner?

What do I do when my offer is countered? Where can I find a person that can help me with testing? What other programs are available to me?" Good real estate agents and loan officers will have the answer to those questions. If they do not know the answers, they should know exactly where to find the answers.

Buying a home doesn't have to be STRESSFUL!

I always say buying a home has many moving parts. If you take a step back and consider all of the components, you have several personalities and functions involved in the transaction. There is the buyer, the seller, the real estate agent, the listing agent, the selling agent, the mortgage loan officer, loan processors and the attorneys and paralegals on both sides.

Put all of these people together, and you have many different personalities and emotions. There are the tense nerves of the buyer and the seller, both wondering if they are doing the right thing. The sellers are emotional over the property they have lived in for so many years, and the buyer is nervous about a huge commitment.

Then there is the bureaucracy of the mortgage lenders with their guidelines and regulations for lending money for the purchase of a property in Massachusetts. All of this happens within strict time constraints, with most transactions occurring quickly between 45 and 60 days. You make an offer on a property, and often, in less than 60 days, you are living in the property. This time flies by quickly with an enormous number of things happening within that brief time. Stressful? Yes, it can be stressful for everyone going through the transaction, especially for the first time.

When you work with a real estate attorney on your side, he or she is an excellent buffer, making sure that the buyer is not distracted by any behind-the-scenes personality conflicts that may be going on. A good real estate attorney can counsel you through this very brief time period, assisting you as you make important decisions throughout the process. Then, when each decision-making occasion arises, you may feel like you were prepared to make an informed decision with much less stress. This is particularly helpful when you understand that aside from the stress of the buyers, the agents are also under enormous pressure to close properties.

It's important to protect the buyer and to be sure the pressure isn't pushed onto them. I see it all the time. Buyer clients will call me saying, "Oh, I have to get that signed. I have to get this signed. We need to do this right away." I tell them, "Wait a second. Step back. Relax for a moment, and think about what your challenge at hand is and how important it is. You don't want to be pressured into doing something only because the seller or the agents are telling you that it needs to be done right away. It's a big decision that you're making, and there's a lot of pressure to begin with." I always tell buyers, "Don't be so anxious to get things done hastily." That is one of the key things to remember as a real estate attorney: be the voice of reason and an advisor to help your buyer clients remain calm and act deliberately instead of at the urging of a lender, agent or seller.

What can go wrong with a closing?

More often than not, when a real estate transaction has problems, it is because the buyer, seller, or both parties did not have proper guidance. Because there are so many moving parts in a real estate transaction, it is critical that those involved fully understand how the process works. Even an experienced buyer or seller won't have all of the know-how to make all of the right decisions that are necessary to avoid simple mistakes.

I have seen many transactions go wrong over the simplest of matters. In most situations, the cause of the problem was one or both parties not having the proper representation. It might have been that they started off trying to do everything by researching the process on the Internet. It also could have been because they got connected with the wrong professionals, like an unqualified internet mortgage lender or an inexperienced real estate agent. Either way, the results are the same. Ultimately, these "professionals" fail to deliver on the promises they make. In the case of an unqualified loan officer, or as I like to refer to them an "absentee loan officer," buyers come to the closing table and find out that the terms that they were expecting are not being met. The lender that they started with has not fulfilled their promises.

You are only a first-time homebuyer once in your life, right? You may have a family member here or there who bought their first house, but when you're going through it for the first time yourself, you're unsure. It is unfamiliar territory during a time when you want the right team guiding you. As someone making the first most significant investment in your life, you want a high quality real estate professional that is trained to help you find the right house in the right neighborhood under the right terms. You want someone who suits your needs, meets you where you are at this point in your life, and is equipped to advise you to be sure you are considering every detail to assure a perfect transaction.

When you work with a good real estate attorney, he or can paint the proper picture of the expectations. As a professional, he or she can provide you with a timeline that outlines exactly what to expect in the process. As the professional on your behalf, he or she should be clear about what you can anticipate throughout the entire transaction. When all you have is advice from the Internet, no one is truly accountable to make sure the process goes smoothly, and no one is available to quell your anxiety. This is where working with the right real estate agent is critical.

I can't stress enough how important it is to have the right team. When working with me, you have the benefit of a full team with each member possessing his or her own expertise. The Realtor® is going to help you find the property that you want. The home inspector is going to inspect the property. The loan officer is going to make sure you are financed properly. The closing attorney is going to tie it all together to ensure that the legal details of the transaction are addressed. Like I often say, real estate is a team sport, a full-contact sport, and the team approach should be taken very seriously.

Situations that are out of the buyer's control tend to create the most problems. The most frustrating are seller or lender delays. Perhaps the sellers cannot move out on time, or for some other reason the seller is unable to perform and deliver the property according to the terms of the agreement. Obviously, if the lender's appraisal shows a value less than the purchase price, that will create an issue, one completely out of the buyer's control. An unexpected failure of a septic system inspection can result in a delay that could completely derail the transaction.

I would not say these examples are common, but if a buyer is unprepared for such delays, it can be very upsetting and put the buyer in a difficult position. If a seller is unable or unwilling to perform and breaks the contract, a buyer's remedies are limited. They may get their deposit back, or they may bring a law suit against the seller and demand performance. Practically speaking, however, forcing a seller to perform is difficult, expensive, and time-consuming.

The same is true for lender delays, there are a multitude of issues that may cause a lender to delay or derail a closing. Though less common, when a lender fails to perform, recourse against them is also limited.

Knowing your closing costs?

Your loan program will determine your closing costs, which usually consist of lender charges for appraisal, credit report, discount points, flood certification fees, and tax service fees, as well as private mortgage insurance and application fees. Other costs that can be considered closing costs are attorney or settlement fees, title charges, and adjustments.

The funds a borrower needs to bring to closing often include other costs and expenses that are overlooked. Items such as real estate taxes that will be due or adjusted at the time of closing, municipal services for municipal light and power, trash and sewer services, and condominium fees, if the property is a condominium ownership or an association of some sort, will need to be accounted for. These costs will be adjusted at closing, and the total of costs comprises the cash you will need to bring to closing. These fees range from around $1,000 to $3,000, depending on the loan program and the transaction. It is always good to know what the costs are and what the total is up front. It is fairly easy for your team to help you determine a solid estimate of what the total will be.

What is a closing cost credit?

A closing cost credit is a type of credit that a seller can give a buyer. The amount of the credit is intended to assist the buyer with closing costs associated with their mortgage loan. This type of credit is something that the buyer may negotiate with the seller at the time the offer is made. Essentially, the buyer would offer to pay the seller a certain amount more than what the buyer is willing to pay as a purchase price, provided that the seller gives the buyer a credit back for the same amount. For example, if you are willing to make an offer of $150,000 for the property but would like a $5,000 closing cost credit to help cover your closing costs, then you would offer $155,000 and include a term in the initial offer to purchase that the seller credits you $5,000 towards your closing costs at closing. Increasing your offer, or increasing the selling price by the amount of the credit, shouldn't affect the seller's bottom line or net, and it allows the buyer to pay less up front on closing costs associated with the mortgage loan. This way, the buyer comes to the closing table with less money required than they would have needed without the arrangement because they are including that money into the mortgage, minus whatever amount they are putting down on the purchase.

If you do not request a closing cost credit in the initial offer, and you are later not satisfied with the results of your home inspection (and I always recommend a home inspection), then you may consider requesting a closing cost credit from the seller as a way to compensate for the issues with the home inspection. This is provided that the seller refuses or is not able to address any home inspection issues directly or provide some other concession.

As a buyer, you need to remember that you can request any kind of credit or concession from the seller, and the seller may agree to it, but it is ultimately up to the mortgage lender to decide if the credit or concession from the seller is acceptable. It is also important to understand that if the seller does agree to a closing cost credit and your closing costs do not total the amount of the credit, your lender may not allow you to receive the full agreed upon credit from the seller, essential leaving money on the table to the seller's benefit. The "seller closing cost credit" language of the purchase and sale agreement is likely to be phrased to indicate that the seller will only give a credit "up to" the agreed upon amount. So, if the seller agrees to give a $2,500.00 closing cost credit, and your actual closing costs only total $2,000.00, your lender will not likely allow you to get the full credit from the seller. The seller will not be obligated to credit, or otherwise pay you, the difference. This frustrating situation is not uncommon, it is just a risk the buyer needs to understand and accept in advance.

Certain lending standards and compliance regulations may not allow for any seller credits at all. It's the lender who will determine whether the option is viable for the particular situation. In a situation such as a closing cost credit, the best way to know your options is to discuss them with your mortgage lender representative or qualified real estate attorney.

Should you have a pre-approval?

It is a good idea to get a pre-approval for mortgage financing early in the home buying process. Many real estate agents will not consider working with buyers who do not have a pre-approval of some sort, and many others will insist that the buyer obtain a pre-approval from a recognized or specific lender. This is because experienced agents have learned not to waste time with unqualified borrowers. A pre-approval simply states that you are pre-approved to purchase up to a certain amount. It is not a commitment from the lender to make the loan. It simply states that based on certain information provided (but not verified) the buyer may qualify for a loan. Most pre-approvals are not particularly reliable, and frankly, many agents and sellers know it. Still, they want to see that a potential buyer has taken the time and effort to go through the process to at least consider what they could afford.

What is really important, though, is the actual commitment from a lender. Working with a local lender that provides this pre-approval statement communicates that you are pre-approved to borrow a certain amount, and it buys you credibility.

This is particularly true if the lender and loan officer is familiar to the agent. If you should wind up in a competitive bidding on a piece of property, you want to make sure you have a pre-approval that's going to stand up. Sellers and agents are going to look at a borrower who has a pre-approval from a local lender with an established reputation, as opposed to a pre-approval from Big Bank of the West that the seller or real estate agent has never heard of. The real estate agent may not encourage the seller to accept such an offer with all things considered. Gaining this local lender pre-approval can prevent incident of having to go through the whole process, only to have it all fall apart, and needing to begin over again because they have the wrong (unqualified) buyer.

Does it matter what day of the month you close?

It is a fallacy that it makes a critical difference to close at the end of the month. Homebuyers often push to close at the end of the month because they believe they will save some money. The reason for closing at the end of the month has been misunderstood, and the confusion has to do with mortgage interest and when it may or may not be paid. No matter when you close, whether you close on the 15th of the month or the 30th, you're still paying prepaid interest on the transaction to the mortgage lender for the period of time between the actual first payment and the date of closing.

Ultimately, if you close towards the end of the month, you may save a little bit of per diem, or daily, interest, but you're going to be paying it anyway with the subsequent mortgage payment. It is important to understand that mortgage payments, unlike rent payments, are paid in arrears. That is a payment due on the first of June is actually for the month of May, and the July payment is for the month of June, and so on. If you close on the 18th of the month, you will pay about 12 days of prepaid interest to the lender at closing. Whereas, if you close on the 30th, you will pay only one or two days of per diem interest.

If you close the first week of June, June 4 for example, you will pay interest at closing for 26 days with the first regular payment due August 1. The cash required at closing would be higher than if you closed in late May, but the first payment would be pushed out almost a month.

Alternatively, you may be able to close June 4 and receive an interest credit at closing for 4 days with the first monthly payment due July 1. The cash required at closing would be lower in this example, but you would pay a full month's interest on July 1 even though you did not have the loan for a full month.

The bottom line is that there is no significant financial advantage in closing on any one day of the month over another. In fact, with so many people trying to close at the end of the month, it can create a hectic time for real estate professionals. Most closing attorneys are the busiest during the last two or three days of the month and the first two or three days of the month. It can be very stressful and demanding while we are working with buyers who are excited to close, to get transactions done, and to move into the property. Most of whom are trying to meet deadlines to vacate their current living arrangements.

Closing in the middle of the month makes a big difference in the amount of stress that a buyer may have. It also makes a big difference in wrapping up their current living arrangement. For example, if they are renting a property, they will likely have to give notice to their landlord in advance. When the closing is scheduled for the middle of the month, they afford themselves a week or two to move out of their current living arrangement in to their new home. This effectively eliminates the pressure of a time restraint of closing on the 30th and vacating by the 1st. Closing on the 30th to be out on the 1st leaves little time to pack and be out of the former dwelling and into the new home.

A word about mortgage insurance (PMI)

According to statistics compiled by the mortgage industry, borrowers who contribute less than 20% of their own money towards the purchase of real estate are more likely to default on payment than borrowers who contribute more. To protect against the risk of default by borrowers who put down less than 20%, mortgage lenders can obtain an insurance policy. This type of insurance policy is referred to as private mortgage insurance, also known as PMI. As a condition of making the loan, a lender will require that the buyer pay the premium for the cost of the policy coverage. If the borrower ends up walking away from their obligation and defaulting on payments, the mortgage insurance company would pay out and cover the lender's losses. So, the only time you would need mortgage insurance is if you're putting less than 20% of the value of the property down towards the purchase of the property. The good news is that mortgage insurance enables a buyer to purchase a property without having to come up with a large down payment. Mortgage insurance is often considered "necessary evil," but it often means the difference between being able to purchase and not.

Can you get your initial "good faith" deposit back?

There's no hard and fast rule. If I'm representing the buyers, I'm going to encourage them to put as little down as possible for a good faith deposit. More often than not, the initial deposit is going to be $500 to $1,000 with the offer. Upon signing the purchase and sale agreement it is usual and customary that a total of 3% to 5% of the purchase price would be paid. There are some exceptions, but to be competitive in a landscape of competing with multiple offers, the more you put down, the more it shows the seller that you have "skin in the game" and that you have made a commitment to them. When you play it safe with deposits, putting down as little as possible is not bad advice, but to be practical, it's optimum to put down upwards of 3% in most circumstances.

If a buyer defaults under the terms of the offer to purchase or under the terms of the purchase and sales agreement (effectively breaching the contract), the buyer will likely lose the deposit as a result. If the buyer performs in accordance with the contract and as agreed, the deposit will be applied to the purchase price at the time of closing. So, don't put down a large initial good faith deposit if you are not willing to lose it in the event you cannot perform under the terms of the contract.

What happens if the home inspector uncovers something you don't expect?

I always recommend having a home inspection done by a professional home inspector. I suggest buyers avoid having an uncle, a cousin, or any relatives or friends in the trades inspect the property for them. A seasoned and experienced home inspector is going to know what to look for and what to disclose, and they are less likely to overlook something that a less experienced professional might. That being said, some home inspectors are better than others. Some will point out every little problem with the property. Others will only point out big issues. It is wise to get a referral for a home inspector that you feel comfortable with and trust.

Ultimately, there's no guarantee that a home inspector is going to uncover every little problem. There is a good chance that they may miss some sort of latent or hidden defect on the property. If this happens, you will not likely have any recourse against the home inspector for not discovering or not disclosing the issue. Most of the time, unless it's a case of gross negligence, the home inspector's liability is going to be limited to the cost of the inspection, which may range from $350 to $500, depending on the particulars of the property and inspection options. But a home inspection IS very important. The inspector can help you find things that are wrong with the property that either the seller doesn't know about, did not disclose, or was aware of but did not consider as a problem.

If a problem is identified, the buyer can try to negotiate with the seller for a concession of some sort. Some of the choices are to abandon the transaction, to insist the seller repair the issue prior to closing, to request a credit from the seller for repair, or to request a reduction in the sale price. Whatever is agreed upon, the details of the agreement should be included in the purchase and sale agreement. Be aware that if there are significant issues with the condition of the property, your mortgage lender may impose conditions upon the completion of the repairs, and often these conditions can be unreasonable and costly.

What's included, what's not?

As a general rule, appliances are usually included, depending on what's disclosed in the listing; however, appliances are not generally considered real estate fixtures.

More often than not, they are included as part of the sale price. Real estate fixtures are defined as anything that is physically attached to the property. A rule of thumb that works is "If it takes a hammer, screwdriver, wrench or some other tool to remove it, then it's likely a fixture."

As with most things, there are some grey areas such as wall mount TV's. Certainly, if you can get the TV off the mount easily, the TV is personal property, and it's not included. However, the mount on the wall could arguably be considered a fixture. It is always best to clarify any unclear or questionable items up front.

It is possible to pay the seller an amount above and beyond the purchase price for a couch, living room set, dining room, or anything else that would not necessarily be considered a fixture. It is just a matter of negotiating the details.

I had a situation, one time, where a seller had inherited property with an old 1,500-pound furnace in the basement. It was practically impossible to remove because the property was renovated around it. The boiler was ultimately unhooked and abandoned in place when the owner installed a new, high efficiency system.

He lived on the property for years before he decided to sell, but he never included or excluded the old furnace as part of the sale. The new buyers presumed that the old furnace was not part of the sale and that it would be removed.

When the buyers did their walk-through prior to closing, there was the old 1,500-pound cast-iron furnace still in the basement. The buyers refused to proceed with the closing if the furnace was not removed. The seller considered it a fixture, but the buyers did NOT. The seller was forced to hire a company to torch the furnace apart and remove it piece by piece.

I have also seen issues arise over misunderstandings over children's play sets, trampolines, above-ground swimming pools, hot-tubs, smart thermostats, small sheds, solar panels, wood piles, engine blocks, and anvils, flat screen television mounts; the list goes on. Never assume ANYTHING in a transaction.

It is also important to understand that when a property is being sold "as is" the term refers to the condition of the property at the time of the offer and inspection of the property. So, don't think that you are obligated to accept the property that has been damaged in between the date of the offer/inspection and date of closing. I once had a very upset buyer call me to explain that the house that he was contracted to close on in a week had a truck drive through the front of it the evening before. He had agreed to buy the property "as is," and now the front porch was destroyed and there was a truck-size hole where the front door used to be. I assured him if the house was not in that condition on the date of his home inspection that he would not be obligated to close on the property in that condition. "As is" or not.

What is a homeowner's warranty?

Sometimes, in an enticement to purchase the property, the seller will offer to pay a home warranty or a third-party vendor that provides a warranty on the systems and the mechanics of the property. The purpose of such a warranty is to cover a new home owner in the event there is a defect with the water pipes, electricity, appliances, or any system covered under the particular policy. Often, the policies I see contain so many exceptions to coverage, it almost doesn't make it worth purchasing the policy. If a seller is going to pay for it and provide it to you, then by all means, take it, but I wouldn't recommend making your decision to buy the property based on whether or not a warranty is being offered.

The mortgage survey

A mortgage survey is service that a lender will require to be done on the property. If you are paying cash for a property, you should also have a mortgage survey performed, but it is not required. The survey, also known as a plot plan, is used to make sure that the foundation of the property sits within the boundary line. It also helps to determine whether or not there may be encumbrances by the neighbors. If an abutting property has a structure that appears to go over the property line, a survey may reveal such an encroachment.

A mortgage survey does NOT show where the boundary lines are on the ground. It is an approximation of where the engineer believes the boundary lines for the property are located. Although the engineer may visit the property, they may not bring any surveying tools or instruments along to do the survey. Often, the survey is completed just by viewing the property layout and following up with a look at the municipal and land records to verify that they have studied the correct property. This process provides enough information for the engineer to determine where the boundary lines are in reference to the foundation and that the foundation is within those boundary lines. The plot plan may also identify whether or not the property is in a flood zone or subject to easements or rights-of-way.

Occasionally, a mortgage survey may reveal that a structure encroaches or appears to encroach over a boundary line. If an encroachment of permanent structures exists, it can be costly and time-consuming to resolve. Other issues identified by a mortgage survey may be minor or less complicated to resolve. Mortgage surveys are not required for condominiums.

What you should know about flood and hazard insurance

Flood insurance, though beneficial, can be very expensive. If the property you are purchasing is in a certain type of flood zone, the cost of that flood insurance policy is figured into your debt-to-income ratio, which helps to determine whether or not you can actually afford the monthly cost of your principal, interest, taxes, insurance, flood insurance, and private mortgage insurance, if necessary.

Knowing whether or not the property you are considering is in a flood zone is important, as well as understanding the risks and the costs associated with it. More often than not, the seller will know if the property is in a flood zone that requires flood insurance. The seller will usually disclose it if they are aware of it, but I have seen instances where a seller is unaware or doesn't disclose it, and the buyer finds out late in the process. Because of the expense of flood insurance, finding out too late in the process can be detrimental. As part of their due diligence, the lender will obtain a flood certification for every property they lend money on. That certification will tell the lender if the property is in a flood zone that requires insurance. If the property requires flood insurance, it will be the borrower's responsibility to pay for the cost of the insurance and maintain the coverage over the life of the loan.

Hazard insurance is completely different from flood insurance. Most homeowner's insurance will not cover natural disaster types of floods. Hazard insurance is just another name for homeowner's, or property and casualty insurance, which covers the property in the event of a fire, if there is other damage, or if somebody slips and falls on the property. Just about any kind of casualty that could be suffered on the property would be covered under the homeowner's insurance policy; this policy should not be confused with the title insurance or flood insurance.

Hazard insurance is also required by a mortgage lender, and it is the borrower's responsibility to pay the premium and maintain coverage. A lender may require that you escrow the cost of the insurance and pay the monthly premium for the policy as part of your monthly mortgage payment. Be certain to discuss escrows with your mortgage loan officer. Understanding how escrows work and how they affect your monthly payment can make the closing process easier.

Understanding the title search and title insurance

Whenever title, or ownership, to real estate changes hands, it is critical to check the "chain" or history of ownership. This is primarily to ensure that the seller is the true and lawful owner and that they have the legal right to sell the property. The title examination, or search, is the responsibility of the closing attorney and is completed as part of the closing process to ensure that the seller is conveying a valid, clear title to the buyer (and potentially to the lender). This process certifies that the seller actually owns the property and has the right to convey it to you. It also ensures that the seller will convey the property free from any unexpected liens or encumbrances. The closing attorney is trained to study court records to determine the chain of ownership of a property and to determine what liens or encumbrances may affect the new buyer.

An examination of the title will also reveal defects other than liens and encumbrances. For example, in order for a deed to effectively convey complete ownership of a piece of property, it must be signed by all of the owners and by the spouses of the owners in some cases. If, in the course of transferring title to the property, a vested owner fails to sign a deed, a defect in the chain of title is created. Defects must be resolved before an owner can convey to a new buyer.

The term "clean title" means that anything that might have affected the sale of the property, including defects, have been paid off, discharged, or otherwise resolved.

Title insurance is a type of insurance that protects the owner of a property from claims challenging their ownership rights. Title defects, liens, and encumbrances that have been overlooked can jeopardize a person's legal right of ownership. A title insurance company will defend an insured owner from claims or will compensate an owner for losses sustained as a result of defects in title and disputes in ownership. An example of a defect would be a case where the deed fails to accurately or completely describe the property or portion being conveyed.

Title insurance should not be confused with property insurance, or hazard insurance, which protects the physical structure of the property from damage or other liability. Title insurance protects the legal right of ownership and provides no coverage for physical damage to the property or occupants. Title insurance is also different from flood insurance and private mortgage insurance.

The premium for the cost of title insurance is paid as part of the closing costs, and the title insurance policy is issued upon closing. The cost of an owner's title insurance policy is approximately $4 for every $1,000 of the purchase price. The premium payment is made only once, at the time of closing, and the policy covers the owner for the duration of their ownership.

A buyer or owner is not required to purchase a title insurance policy for their own protection, but a mortgage lender's policy is required. Mortgage lenders are in the business of lending money secured by real estate, and they will not take the risk of closing a loan without the protection of title insurance. Many buyers mistakenly think that because the lender has a policy, they are also covered under that policy as a buyer or owner. What they don't understand is that the lender's title insurance policy is not effective until the lender forecloses on the property and takes it from the owner. That's the only time the lender can make a claim under that policy. If there is a defect on the title and the owner goes to sell the property, a lender's policy will not cover the owner.

If a title defect is discovered during the insured ownership of the property, you have limited options. You can undertake to resolving the defect on your own, you can retain an attorney to resolve it for you, or you can try to bring suit against the former owner or the title attorney. Neither of these options are practical; however, if you have purchased owner's title insurance, you can rely on the policy coverage to protect your interest. Purchasing an owner's title insurance policy is particularly important when buying property that has a complex chain of ownership, when buying newly developed land, and when buying foreclosed property.

It is important to understand that title insurance protects against adverse claims of ownership of the land itself and not necessarily the structure, whether the structure is 100 years of age or newly constructed.

Understanding the Homestead Law

Massachusetts has a homestead law which essentially states that a homeowner's spouse has a legal interest in the ownership of a spouse's primary residence, or homestead. A husband or wife owning a piece of property bearing only his or her name on the title is protected from creditors placing a lien on the property because the spouse also has an interest in that property. This wouldn't apply to a mortgage on the property, but if a homeowner is sued for negligence, failing to pay a debt, or something similar, and a judgment is won against them, the person who owns the judgment (the creditor) can attach the property and force the owners to sell the property to pay the judgment. If the property has been declared as a homestead, then the equity in the property is protected up to $100,000. This means that a creditor cannot force the sale of the property, and even if the property is sold, $100,000 of the equity is protected from the claim of the creditor.

In years past, an application and filing in writing were required. The legislature recently changed the law providing that if it's your primary residence, you have $100,000 worth of equity protection automatically. However, if you do file in writing, the protection goes up to $500,000 of equity protection. You only need to file it once, and you are covered for as long as you own the property as your primary residence.

The need for a "smoke" certificate

According to Massachusetts state law, residential properties are required at the time of conveyance to have been inspected for smoke alarms and carbon monoxide detectors. Generally, it is the seller's responsibility to have the local fire department come through and inspect the property prior to closing. The fire department will check to see that the smoke and carbon monoxide detectors are in working order and are installed in the proper locations. When the property passes the inspection, the fire department will issue a compliance certificate, which will need to be provided to the closing attorney. On occasion, the responsibility of obtaining the certification will be placed on the buyer. The terms of the purchase and sale agreement should indicate who will be responsible to obtain the certificate.

Buying a Home with Solar Panels

If you are considering purchasing a home that has solar panels find out in advance if the panels are owned by the seller or if the seller is leasing them from a solar or utility company. This will make a big difference in their value and any possible complications that may arise prior to closing.

If the panels are owned by the seller, the value of the panels should already be factored into the asking price of the home. Speak with your Realtor® about other homes in your market with panels and that are similar to the home you are considering to determine if the value of the panels on the home is reasonable.

Many solar panel systems, whether leased or owned have the benefit of the value of Solar Renewable Energy Credits (SREC). Panels generate SREC credits and someone is likely receiving the benefit/value of these credits. Every megawatt hour (MWh) of electricity produced by the solar panel system generates an SREC. Utility companies purchase these credits in order to comply with Federal renewable energy mandates. So, the property may benefit from both the electricity generated by the solar array, and by the SREC it generates. However, sometimes, the property owner only receives the benefit of the electricity, and the solar company retains the rights to the value of the SRECs.

Buyers need to understand exactly how they will benefit from the panels. Every system is different, some arrays produce more power than others, some are leased, some are owned outright, and contract terms and conditions vary greatly from one solar vendor to another. If the seller intends to retain any beneficial interest in the panels or in the SERC contract after closing, you must understand how that will affect you as the new owner of the home. Know the particular details of what you are taking on before you enter into a contract to purchase a home with solar panels.

Title 5

"Title 5" refers to a code of the Massachusetts regulations covering sewage disposal systems (310 CMR 15.000), or septic systems, on residential properties. The code states, with few exceptions, that any time a property changes hands, the seller is obligated to have the system inspected and make sure that the buyer is aware of the condition of the system. This protects the buyer from having to replace or repair the system after closing and assures that the system complies with public health along with environmental and conservation standards.

Simply described a septic system receives the waste water from the property, which flows into a system that is self-contained on the property, where the water then leaches back into the earth. These systems have to be maintained and inspected on a regular basis. If you are purchasing a property served by a septic system, you should make it a point to learn as much as you can about how the system works and how they are maintained. Septic systems are expensive to install and repair, and keeping a system in compliance with Title 5 is important to the value of the property.

Title 5 does not apply to property that is connected to a municipal sewer system.

What is a short sale and what should buyers know about it?

The first thing to understand about a short sale is that you are not buying the property from a bank. Just like in a conventional transaction, you are purchasing directly from the owner or seller. However, the owner of the property owes more money to the mortgage holder on the property than the property is actually worth. The seller of the property and their attorney or agent must first obtain permission from the mortgage holder to do this. Getting that permission can be a very time consuming process, and there are certain guidelines that the seller must follow. The seller must get the mortgage lender to agree to take a final payment on the mortgage of less then what is due. For example, a seller owes $295,000 on their mortgage, but the home is only worth $250,000. In order to sell the property, the lender would need to agree to a $45,000 loss. In almost every case, the seller is not allowed to receive any proceeds from the sale and may even need to bring money to the closing in order to complete the sale.

If you are buying a short sale property for the first time, working with a real estate team is especially important because there are even MORE moving parts. Buyers need to understand that a short sale transaction is never final until the date of the closing. Most lenders who are taking a loss reserve the right to rescind the agreement right up to the date of closing. That means you could lose the transaction and valuable time at the very last minute without any recourse. An experienced buyer's agent, or a real estate attorney, can advise the buyer about what the seller is required to do. However, short sale transactions can drag out 60, 90, 120 days, or more. So if you are anxious to get into a property within a certain amount of time, you cannot rely on the terms of a short sale transaction.

<u>Be sure that you plan accordingly, keep a flexible work schedule as much as possible, and make certain you have a place to go or a place to remain in the event the closing is delayed. Consider scheduling movers and giving notice to your landlord only after you have closed.</u>

Do you have a house to sell before you can buy a new one?

Once again, having the right team of professionals to assist and advise you is huge, particularly when you are in a situation where one transaction is, or should be, contingent on the other. If you have an agent listing your property, and they're helping you buy as well, that's great because they're going to know what you need to do for your purchase. They also will know what is happening at the back end of your sale. This is fairly easy if you are selling locally. If you are selling in Kansas and you are relocating to Massachusetts, it is possible you will end up with two different agents—one listing and selling your property in Kansas and one helping you buy in Massachusetts. As long as the communication is there and everybody understands that you have a house to sell before you can be obligated to purchase, it works. You will need to make sure that a contingency goes into any offer that you make or receive on the properties. A contingency should state that your performance as the buyer is contingent upon you selling your home first and actually closing on it. Mortgage home sale contingencies have come across my desk indicating that it is contingent on the seller finding a buyer. Well, it's easy to find a buyer. The difficult thing is the closing.

It is important to know that a contingency could affect your buying of property. It is possible that your offer may not look as attractive as somebody else's offer WITHOUT a contingency. The fewer contingencies in an offer, the more likely the offer is going to be accepted. If you really want to put in a competitive bid, you can remove your financing contingency if you have cash to purchase. You can remove the home inspection contingency if you feel you want to take that risk. If you have property to sell, and you can own two homes at the same time, then you can remove that contingency, but the more you remove, obviously, the more attractive your offer looks.

Contingencies exist to protect you, and when putting them in place, it's good to have the team make sure you have the right contingency written correctly.

How should you prepare for the closing?

The most important thing is for me to try to help my clients understand the process of steps and procedures before it even begins. Even though every transaction is a little different, each buyer goes through the acquisition phase in search of the right property:

- Identifying the right property to purchase
- Making an offer on that property
- Signing a purchase contract
- Getting financing in order
- Meeting lender requirements

Buyers looking for information about the closing process can easily find an unlimited number of resources describing the process on federal government websites, the National Association of Realtors website, and state government websites too. The key point is to understand what is going on and when.

The second most important thing is to be informed of possible delays and to plan accordingly. It's not uncommon to experience delays on a transaction. When you take the day off from work on the day you expect to be closing, it may be necessary to take two or three days in that time period because you may not close on time. If you do not have the pressure of having to get back into the office or punch in for work, it can be helpful. Be flexible. Expect delays.

We had a closing recently where the seller's relocation plans fell through unexpectedly, he literally had no place to go. When the buyers did their walkthrough, the seller had not even packed a single box. But the buyers had given their notice to their landlord and movers had already packed their belongings ready to deliver the next morning. The buyers were understandably upset and angry with the seller. Unfortunately, their recourse was limited. The seller had certainly breached the contract, but to get any sort of judicial relief the buyers would need to bring a law suit against the seller. There was no time for that, not to mention that cost would be extensive. However, after several days of negotiating with the seller's attorney an agreement was worked out and the seller vacated the property. The seller paid the buyers a small sum of money for their trouble, but it did not even cover the daily expense of the moving company.

In addition to expecting delays and planning accordingly, knowing what is expected from you up front before you go to the closing is imperative. Be certain to know the amount of money you are expected to bring to closing. Most closing attorneys will require a certified bank or cashier's check for amounts over $1,000.00. Also bring your personal checkbook for smaller, unexpected costs that may come up at the last minute. Never bring large amounts of cash to closing, most closing attorneys will not accept it. If necessary, you can arrange to make a wire transfer to the closing attorney. Whenever you send a wire in a real estate transaction always double and triple check the instructions for sending the wire. Avoid being the subject of a wire fraud scheme by confirming with the closing attorney that you have the correct wire transfer instructions.

You should also bring with you a state-issued driver's license or photo identification. Some lenders may require an additional form of identification, as well as a copy of a recent pay stub.

The closing attorney will usually send out a letter with a list of what is needed at the closing. Read the letter. If you get anything in the mail in reference to your transaction, whether from the mortgage lender, the Realtor® or an attorney, read it. Read through ALL of it. These are sent for a reason.

Be certain to conduct a walkthrough

The walkthrough is not a home inspection. The home inspection should have been completed well in advance to closing and preferably before signing the purchase and sale agreement. The walk-through is usually conducted by the buyer just prior to closing. It is essentially a physical review of the property just to make sure that the property is being delivered as expected.

No one wants to sit at the closing table and sign to purchase a property that just had a truck drive through the front porch overnight. Without a walk- through, you could possibly sign all the documents, which are then sent to record, and the result is that you now own a property without a front porch and a truck-size hole where the front door used to be. The walk-through is done to make sure that the property has not changed significantly since the time you did your inspection and the time of the closing.
I can't recall how many times a buyer, for one reason or another, has opted not to do a walk-through, only to find out something terrible had happened to the property since the buyer's last visit to the property. It is a buyer's right to conduct a walk-through. Don't pass up that right. Conduct your walk-through as close to the actual closing as possible. The evening before is usually sufficient. This is your chance to be sure that the property is being sold to you "as is" and in the relatively same condition as it was in during your home inspection.

The Closing Disclosure and other closing documents

At closing, you will sign a document known as the Closing Disclosure (CD). Among other details, it will disclose how the funds are being disbursed on the transaction. This document reflects the purchase price, deposits, commissions, taxes that are being paid, recording fees, attorneys' fees, and any payments that have to do with conveyance of the property. By signing the note, you are making a promise to the mortgage lender. You are pledging to pay them back under the certain terms listed in the note. It also indicates that if you break that promise, the lender can foreclose on the property under the terms of the mortgage.

You will also sign a mortgage. The mortgage is a document separate from the note. It is a security agreement for the repayment of the note saying that you have made a written, legal promise to repay the lender. If you don't pay back the lender, the lender can foreclose, under certain conditions, and those conditions are listed out in the mortgage. The most important documents you sign at the closing for the lender are the CD, the note, and the mortgage.

The Closing Disclosure should coincide and agree with the information and details provided on the Loan Estimate. Your lender is required to provide the Loan Estimate to you within three days of having completed your application. You should receive the Closing Disclosure at least three days prior to closing. A majority of the other documents are disclosures and acknowledgements having to do with the terms of the loan and important information about you and the lender.

REO and Non-Conventional Sellers

If you are buying an REO property, it is important to understand that a bank owns the property. "REO" stands for real estate owned, which means it is real estate owned by a bank that made a loan on the property. The bank acquired the property by foreclosing on the buyer who defaulted under the terms of the mortgage, most likely for failing to pay the balance due. When a bank acquires a property this way, the bank adds the property to its inventory and places it for sale to the public to the services of a Realtor®. An REO seller is commonly listed as the bank that held the mortgage, such as Bank of America, Chase, Federal National Mortgage Association or other local bank, lender or credit union.

Regardless of who the selling bank or entity is, buying an REO can be a time-consuming, complicated process. More often than not, an REO buyer will be required to enter into a rather one-sided purchase agreement, and the terms of the agreement will strongly favor the seller. REO agreements leave little recourse against the seller in the event of a seller's default. REO agreements will often require the buyer to pay all, or a portion of, the seller's expenses in addition to the purchase price. This provision often catches buyers off guard. If the REO seller defaults, or otherwise chooses ultimately not to sell the property to the buyer, the buyer's only reasonable remedy would be to reclaim their deposit. One of the major important terms to understand in an REO contract is that if the buyer is unable to close on time, the buyer may be subject to a daily payment of up to a hundred dollars per day.

Although real estate owned contracts favor the seller, they are usually very liberal with providing the buyer inspection contingencies. Take every opportunity to have an REO property professionally inspected as soon as possible. Understand that REO sellers will disclaim all responsibility for property condition and will not likely agree to repairs or concessions.

If you are STILL considering buying a "bank owned" or REO property, know that the closing may not occur on the contracted closing date. Unfortunately, as stated, these types of transactions can be complicated and time consuming and are often subject to frustrating and costly delays. Be sure that you plan accordingly, keep a flexible work schedule as much as possible, and make certain you have a place to go or a place to remain in the event the closing is delayed. Consider scheduling movers and giving notice to your landlord only after you have closed.

David Rocheford: My Final Words

When I meet with a home buyer for the first time, it is usually by phone call. The real estate timeline of transactions is speedy; rapport-building is something that happens quickly between me and my clients. Our first call typically lasts between 30 and 45 minutes—whatever it takes to help us become acquainted.

I wrote this book to help educate people about some of the pitfalls in the homebuying process and more importantly, about how a real estate attorney as part of your team can prevent a disaster. To show my gratitude for reading my book and helping me to leverage my time, I am offering you a special gift. My hourly rate is $275 yet I am happy to waive the $206.25 fee for our 45-minute consultation to help you understand the entire process. **The time is mine and the price is FREE.**

Buying a home is one of the most rewarding, yet significant decisions of your life. If you are in the market for a new home, I urge you to make an appointment with me. It won't cost you a dime, yet what you can learn can save you thousands of dollars, many sleepless nights and infinite stress. When we get together, I will share everything I can about the process, answer your questions and help you feel completely confident and comfortable about process.

I look forward to helping you take those satisfying steps toward becoming a property owner with the security of knowing a legal advisor is looking out for your best interests. Call me today, and we can begin your house-hunting journey together.

David

Find out from others how David Rocheford helped them have the
BEST CLOSINGS:

"David and the entire team at his office were outstanding in helping me through my real estate purchase. We discovered problems during our final walk through of the property and what could have been an absolute nightmare for my wife and me was resolved swiftly and professionally. Thank you all for getting me and my wife into our new home."

Denis L. – Westminster, MA

"I contacted attorney Rocheford to assist me in my real estate purchase. David was very reassuring during our initial consultation and his office made me feel very at ease with the whole process. I received updates as and when necessary, so I knew where I stood in the process the entire time. I would not hesitate to use his office again when I buy or sell my next home."

Susan M. – Worcester, MA

"What a top notched attorney! David agreed to assist me with 2 days' notice of a signing date and everything was pulled together beautifully without hesitation. David and team did an outstanding job and ended up closing on my purchase ahead of schedule! Potential delays on the seller's side were handled without missing a step! I highly recommend him to anyone who is in the process of buying real estate. Excellent response time, very knowledgeable and someone who will gladly assist you."

Howard M. – Princeton, MA

Buying Real Estate in Massachusetts

Work with us to experience the BEST CLOSING of your NEW PROPERTY!

Call my office today:

978-728-5104

www.TheBestClosings.com/BuyerBook

Call to secure your

FREE 45-MINUTE CONSULTATION

(A $206.25 value)

WE have helped more than 9,500 property buyers have a PROFESSIONAL and SMOOTH closing!

Make our team a part of YOUR team!

Or let us introduce you to a qualified real estate agent and mortgage loan officer!

We help guide you through the entire process!

Your NEW home AWAITS YOU!

 **David R. Rocheford, Jr.** has been involved in real estate for over 20 years. First as a real estate agent while attending college at night. Later David worked as a paralegal and as an intern for a busy real estate law office while attending law school. After graduating, David started his own practice and dedicated himself to becoming an expert in real estate matters. He has been involved in well over 7,000 real estate transactions and his practices represents banks, mortgage lenders, buyers and sellers. Having experienced firsthand the common mistakes that adversely affect his buyer clients, this book is intended to help home buyers recognize some of the mistakes to avoid.

www.ingramcontent.com/pod-product-compliance
Lightning Source LLC
Chambersburg PA
CBHW070407190526
45169CB00003B/1154